THE BURDEN OF BEING BURMESE

THE BURDEN OF BEING BURMESE

Poems by **KO KO THETT**

Zephyr Press | **mccm**creations

Published in 2015 by
Zephyr Press www.zephyrpress.org
MCCM Creations www.mccmcreations.com

Dedication from *The Burman, His Life and Notions*
by Shway Yoe (1889), translated by ko ko thett

Cover photograph by Andrew Rowat
Book design by typeslowly
Printed in Hong Kong

Frontis image:
36 animals by Htein Lin / *Myanmar Encyclopedia*
36 animals is a roulette-like game, a staple at pagoda festivals in Burma / Myanma

Author photograph:
ko ko thett reciting poetry in a school competition in the
Socialist Republic of the Union of Burma (ca. 1979) by San Lwin (Prome)

I am profoundly grateful to the editors and staff members of the following journals and anthologies for acknowledging my work: *The Wolf, World Literature Review, Washington Square Review, Warscapes, Postscript, PN Review, Tuli & Savu, International Times, International Gallerie, English PEN magazine, Cold Noon Travel Poetics, Bengal Lights, Asia Literary Review, Axon, The Wolf (A Decade: Poems from 2002–2012)* edited by James Byrne (2012), *Poetry for Peace for Amnesty International* by Michael Lidgley and Devanshe Chauhan (2015), *CAPITALS* by Abhay K. (2015) and *Mountain, River and Steppe: Ecopoetries from Eastern Asia* by Mark Bender (2016).

Special thanks to Soe Naung Thaw, Lut Lams, Kenton Clymer, Kelly Falconer and Christopher Mattison for their love, inspiration and, above all, patience.
Zephyr Press acknowledges with gratitude the financial support of the Massachusetts Cultural Council.

massculturalcouncil.org

Published with support from the SOMA Project, City University of Hong Kong

Cataloguing-in publication data is available from the Library of Congress.

ISBN 978-1-938890-16-1 (US)
ISBN 978-988-13114-5-0 (HK)

TABLE OF CONTENTS

အံ့ပဲသြသြ၊ သဘောပဲ ကျကျ ဗမာလူမျိုးဆိုတာ 'အမေ့'
လို့တလေ့ရှိတယ်။ ဗမာထုံးစံမှာ အမေဟာ အခရာမို့
ဒီစာအုပ်နဲ့ ကန်တော့လိုက်ပါတယ် ချစ်တဲ့ အမေ။
အချီးကျူးသန်၊ အဝေဖန်နု၊ အချော့အသိမ့် သိမ်မွေ့၊
အကာအကွယ်ပေးဖို့ အမြဲအသင့်ဖြစ်တဲ့နေရာမှာ အမေ့ကို
ဘယ်သူမှမမီတာမို့ ဒီစာအုပ်ဟာ အမေ့အတွက်။
အမေ့ကျေးဇူးကို ဒီလို ရိုသေလေးစားရခြင်းကြောင့် အမေ
တစ်ရက်ပျော်နိုင်တယ်ဆိုရင်ပဲ သားအတွက် ကုသိုလ်ပေါ့အမေ။

ရွှေရိုး [ဗမာလူမျိုး၊ ဘဝနဲ့အယူအဆ]

When anything surprises or pleases a Burman he never fails to cry out, Amé—mother. Following the national example, to whom can I better dedicate this book than to you, my dear Mother? Who else will be so eager to praise; so tender to chide; so soft to soothe and console; so prompt to shield and defend? To you, therefore, I dedicate it; and if this tribute of reverence and gratitude gives you a day's pleasure, it will have been a kaung-hmu—a work of merit.

Shway Yoe [*The Burman, His Life and Notions*]

to the navel of the earth

["auspicious victory" highway bus terminus, yangon]

a great white in a mousetrap
a year of monsoons in twelve hours
a canonball for a stick insect
a peasant girl hawks trifles
doesn't an elephant cut her own path
trampling through the jungle
she won't take no for an answer
sure you don't need a nausea inhaler
i will now drop my appeal
may i have a tissue packet

[crony & co. stopover, 105 miles]

at the roadside cafe *samsara*
someone sits at the end of daily agita

"right view, right intention, right speech,
right action, right livelihood, right effort,
right mindfulness, right concentration"

right on . . .
he used to flex those noble eightfold tentacles
as he is dunked in red pepper sauce
mr. octopus squirts and squirms
all his suction cups beg for existence

[murmuration over the abode of kings, naypyidaw]

what a display of haywires

over the capital's "capital hypermarket"
a battalion of glossy starlings performs
"shadow puppets in search of a new lord"

do your do's and don'ts connect
do the wind and weather help
does an individual ever count

each timeless lick lasts a millisecond
at the expense of the gated sky

[a charity appeal for avīci wells, the red earth hillock]

burmese medium school,   that's where i learned to
speak ghost, a language that never makes you feel good
about sex,   we always go out in a hard hat for fear of
a collapsing sky,   we wear steel-toe boots for fear of foothold
traps,   we will tear down the scaffold once the stupa is set
this country was once occupied by the britishers,   it's now
been colonized by bottled water, donate now for avīci wells

[thousands, millions, gazillions]

leave your comfort and luxury at home
wipe your shoes upon boarding this vehicle
do not put your feet on the aisle seat
do not open the glass windows
we are not responsible for undeclared goods
eating rice on this bus is strictly forbidden
the driver doesn't necessarily know the time of arrival
no smoking, please help with cleanliness
buddha, dhamma, sangha
have a most pleasant travel

panning for alluvial gold
[at the confluence of her dreams]

moving again
aren't we getting tired of our travels
cloudlets, the color of gold gudgeon scales,
don't you find the constriction of a burmese python reassuring
you might as well catch a grass snake by the tail
father, you always sharpened my pencils with your lathe
your shoulders i used to ride with such joy have now turned into
a pair of mistreated oxen willfully refusing
the cart of my muse

where are we moving to
i don't want to be the new student again in a new school
i don't want new friends, i don't want to learn
a new patois, new manners
the temptation of poisonous mushrooms
locusts, grasshoppers, stick insects, crickets
aren't they the same old pulses from the same old wicker baskets
fat spiders, skinny scarecrows, deep-fried sparrows
chameleons, grilled farm rats, boiled quail eggs
fighting with wild plums for space on a bamboo tray
the six glories of the buddha, jasmine strings,
the chests containing all we have, enormous breasts praying for a son,
milk containers, horoscopes, potsherds,
public executioners, the popularity of instant teas,
the effrontery of pronatalist virtues multiplying at an exponential rate
like the water hyacinths plaguing our lakes . . .

all aboard the choo-choo train tootling along a tortuous terrain
aren't we fed up with his master's voice
the wind-up gramophone, the life *samsara*
where are we going

how i miss them

droll are the fire vigilantes
slumbering by the campfire
the toddy palms poorly dressed in bamboo ladders
padauks in the bud anticipate the *thagyan* rain
the rice seedlings dance *yane* in the breeze
as a white heron waits for fish on just one foot
the crow of the cockerels, the tang of the pickles,
the debate of the sickles, the fragrance of fresh cheroots
the sense of your folklores
the scent of your forelocks . . .

mother, why are you so oddly pensive
why don't you speak
i entreat you

bullhorns in the passing lane

right behind me in the blind spot, someone's
sniffing my tail, since when have you been
in my shadow, discreet as death, silent and
invisible
go ahead, there is the yoke, step back, the cane
strokes, drones overhead, dread underground
there are unexploded ordnance
your shrills thrill no one, who's pickled your suns
who's stolen your pickles, who's designed your
flip-flops, who you slept with last night, who you
vote for tomorrow, who wants to read your bumper
stickers, who cares
don't come too close, keep a safe distance
you don't want your nose to bleed, you don't want
burning bitumen on your belly, my road is not car-
worthy, my car is not road-worthy, my brake lights
do not flash
how's my driving, sir, i have a d-phil in pragmatics
in this land of half-cocked guns, every vehicle is
horse-powered, every road leads to the abode of kings
every moth mound is gilded and worshipped
every monkey is money-mad
you don't have a satellite navigator, you don't have a
tall-tale indicator, you don't have a retro-reflector
you don't have a rearview mirror, you don't have
a proximity sensor, can you really see the road ahead

with your eyes on your temples
as far as the lord of the lane is concerned, there is
no slow down, there is no give way, there is no turn back
his dodge may be a go-around, his gear
irreversible

a few ways to eat a city raw

[when you end up somewhere you don't want to be]

eat it like a durian
eat it like someone who'd puke at the mere mention of a durian
you are marooned on durian island
you despise both its shape and soldier-sock stench
you will wait until you can't wait any longer
eat or die, now you can be the primate you've always been
smash open the thorny husk against a rock
dig your digits deep into the succulent pulp
you don't want to look at it, you don't want to smell it
hold your breath or block your nose
shove the flesh down your throat
you will get used to it

[when you are in transit]

eat it walking like you would a box of noodles
it takes better psychomotor skills than piloting a jet
your fingers have to know your chopsticks
your feet have to know your walk
your mouth has to know your bite
you have to know your way

zebra crossings, red lights, green lights, yellow lights, dogs being walked, bicycles whizzing by, policewomen, window displays, functionalist buildings, fashionable locals . . .

only humans, and a few other alien species, can eat on their feet
locate a bin when your sticks get close to the bottom of the box
trash the empty box, walk on

[when you end up in a remote location with your lover
who has bought you the tickets behind your spouse's back]

you know the scenario
the most pleasurable trip
you've got it gratis
you cherish both the journey and the destination
now you must be a slow tourist

you don't want to hurry and finish your paid annual leave
you won't share it with anyone
you don't want it gone,
you don't want it dognapped by the big bully at home

you must be discreet
if you fail, you'll become an insufferable social outcast
if you succeed, you're a lifelong prisoner of your own secret

[when you aren't sure why you're there in the first place]

eat it like a fish who nibbles but won't take the bait
the bloody piece of earthworm is tempting
unless you want to understand the worm's agony
you don't want to snatch him
you might as well be generous for once

let others go first
see how tightly hooked your snack is
see the line, see the knot, see the float, see the sun,
size up the angler through the rippled shadow of his lure's weight

in this scenario
you may be fed, but you won't be filled

the boomtown

a bottle spins
a rat for protein
a snake rattles
pots and pans for a pawnshop
lunar face for the thoroughfare
rickshaw for the landing vehicle

a tadpole morphs into a mermaid
isn't she just another census entry
you don't want to be weighed down
by the food chain, lectures the dean,
hanging loose between two branches

no soup in a salt crystal
no lamp oil in a sand grain
no sum makes her night
no catch cools her day
no rain fills her ocean stomach
no holds barred for her banquet
no one knows what side they're on
in her flesh and faith and toes
no exasperation unbearable
no exile banishment

a nip at the wrong ear, game over
a turn into the wrong lane, you're dead
mahogany doesn't live in a tundra

ghost orchids don't grow in a desert
between winter and summer
spring is the suspender belt

neon trenches for canonical gospels, trains
loaded with final holdouts leave every second
transmigration passes available for non-nationals
how would you like to be wrapped

vicuña wool for your majesty
foliage for the naked

chaos clock

the city's streets are ideal
for both trishaws and sport utility vehicles
motorcycles have been banned,
but you can still tear around town in a helmet

art is cheap, but not available to everyone
the old leafy tree on campus has endured
more than a powerful cyclone, she has finally
lived up to her name, she's now truly rotten

no one escapes the panopticon, no one cares
don't worry about yourself
our clinics supply the intolerably rich with aphrodisiacs and antihypertensives
our pharmacies provide betel and beedies to the filthy poor
everything is for sale
wealth is health

generators in the alleys are busiest
street vendors who used to sell falafel or rice noodles
have found bootlegging dvds more profitable
teenage couples who used to date on the breezy banks
of the city's lakes have checked into its new hotels

the lion sejant in the shades of white and green
will remind you of a sub-saharan political sunset
erstwhile colonial buildings have been colonized by
neo-colonial scarecrows, thatched huts have been

upgraded into residential flats, the monsoon has
flushed away all the stray cats

the muddy serpentine river that once swallowed
whole "the progressive peace" overloaded with
two thousand crabby commuters sludges on
as if nothing happened

in times like these
the associational life is quite beneficial
for a flock of seagulls, flying rats

just beyond nightfall
beside the golden sheldrake on the royal lake
the most exotic mammals come under the hammer of animalism
the starting price, if you ask,
is just u.s. twenty-five hundred
once the *power light* is cast on the display cabinet
sale items, dressed in poverty and virgin virtue, vie for the highest bidder
they will make the best of their three-month contract
practice safe sex, prostitution is illegal

massage parlors are new age churches
where you go to confess your venial sins,
so you can commit them all over again
soon you will be forgiven and forgotten

as the three wit-crackers at their wit's end
begin to grope for fresh gags below the waistline
"don't get lost in the labyrinth of lust"

warns the petite dancer from the limelight, to no effect
as far as the broken mirror in a ktv lounge
in the shadow of shwedagon is concerned,
"smile and i'll smile back"

cockfights used to be popular here
the blood sport is barbaric
people now have other options
scorecasting is not a zero-sum game
investment is pouring in, reeking draws fruit flies
ricky draws angles

there's no municipal services to collect your moral trash
every cup of tea in town grows more bitter each day
of course you can sweeten your life with *ajinomoto*
you can get your visa on arrival

people are welcome, problems are not
living is expensive but dying doesn't cost a dime
where else in the world can you enjoy a free funeral
next thursday isn't auspicious
the dragon's tail is pointing toward your head
would you like to reschedule your appointment

take a look, sir
it's amazing how this victorian clock keeps movement
her minute hand and hour hand are stuck neck and neck
the roman numerals on her face have long faded
did you say "not working"
how much would you pay

wait a moment, sir
can you hear it . . .
tick .... tack, tick ...... tack, tick ... tack

at a cantonese restaurant
a toothpick who knows perfectly
the ingress and egress of the city muses
"billionaires in other places are full of debt
here we only save gold bullion and hard cash"

business as usual
everyone smiles the smile
everything looks just fine
since when did the strife end?

welcome to the fort town of ba htoo

greets the heavily armed army checkpoint
colonel ba htoo died fighting the japanese in the last world war
the town that honors the anti-fascist hero is a purpose-built
breeding ground for the ultra-nationalist myanmar army
where can you find better irony

"basic training" is where boys my age get routinely dehumanized
you're in the *tatmadaw* now
leave all your self, pride and shame outside
run faster, you rat-fucked mother fuckers
are you a girl? go wear a *tamain*
don't you know which of your legs is the right?

attention! why are you here?
for the people, sir, for the people, sir
what kind of spirit do you have?
steel spirit, sir, steel spirit, sir
even steel spirit melts under pressure

private san aung made a suicide pact with his girlfriend
too bad he shot himself first
his chest was sewn up like a gunny sack after the autopsy
flowers, tears, empathy and hypocrisy
went with him down "the bagan road" to the cemetery
for he had fallen in love, not in war,
san aung didn't get a military rite

near ba htoo, the river *wizard* is being dammed
the caucasian engineers climb up the pylons, checking their cables and wires
children play war games, hide-and-seek and fly their kites on a vast plain
where thousands of felled trees await departure

in ba htoo, the pop-pops of daily shooting practice compete with the death
calls of cicadas, in ba htoo, spent mortar shells are reborn as vases for
buddhist shrines and pagodas, in ba htoo, the deafening "charge!" of mock
battles are taken for granted; they no longer induce hysteria, in ba htoo,
rationed "army rum" is always scarce; it's good for malaria, in the monsoon
the *pain* creek eats children and calves, the steep, longish narrow *pain* dries up
in the summer

in ba htoo, everyone suffers from adjustment disorder
no resident is permanent, early retirement is out of the question
quitters are to be shot, life is simply *dukkha*

lawksawk

next to ba htoo is lawksawk,
the little town must have been there forever,
far too long to know
who'd given her that moniker

lawksawk had seen better days
she used to have her own chieftains, the *saophas*
she is now ruled by the township law and order restoration council
she is the town of *shan* enchantresses, bicycle and watch repairers,
forgotten pensioners and affordable tailors
poet thein than htun calls her home
shan, bama, danu, innthar, the tribal populaces mingle and mix
chaw suu htway lives near the bazaar

on weekends, the *tatmadaw* cadets from ba htoo,
freshly powdered faces in exorbitantly pressed uniforms and
excessively polished shoes,
in posses of three to five, haunt lawksawk

they walk in formation, they talk in formation
they even woo lawksawk girls in formation
call it "command recreation" if you dare

the creepy "spiral ladder" temple, the monastery,
the mosque, the state high school, the court and houses of the belles
you'll find every single significant building on a hillock in lawksawk
for a piece of rangoon, a taste of mandalay,

an imitation *taung gyi*, or even a mini *mawlamine*
you go to the teashops along the main road
yet nothing beats lawksawk's own flavor
try steamy hot tofu at the three shan sisters'

at dawn on market days
shoulders yoked with loads of produce,
palaung, *danu* and *pa-o*, peasants from the mountain tribes
come together in lawksawk
arriving at the market in chauffeur-driven willys are
the uppity army officers' wives
dressed in batik, draped in gold, jades and rubies,
the ladies bargain with the day's traders

"slash-and-burn" fascinates me
when the shan mountains burn in the distance
you see a fire dragon dance
the monster moves for nights on end
until it's subdued by a shower

wildlife is treasure
a tiger skin equals a toyota pickup, a scooter for a bear,
would you like a quartz for a tortoise shell
even porcupine spikes adorn your hair

the annual *phayagyi* festival is fun
it happens when the stupa gets floodlit by a diesel *tabota*
as soon as the loudspeakers blare in the evenings
the whole town comes out like a swarm of bees poked from a hive

some kids want to try ferris wheels, powered by the monkey men
some cry for candy floss, conjured up by the magicians

at least a boy will fall from a height
ouch! my left wrist is broken? did you say both radius and ulna?
how did it happen? it hurts like hell! can you straighten it again?
more morphine please, dr. bonesetter

grown-ups shop, compare notes and piss on each other
don't you tease that girl, she *is* my sister!
novices! don't hold back, hedge your bets on the casino mat
be warned, the abbot will flog you if he knows where you are
have you reserved your place in front of the stage for the outdoor
burmese theatre?
dress up, stay warm, take the wool blanket with you, or
snuggle up to your girlfriend

every three years or so
bitter fog kills our agriculture
just bring me some water, i don't want to hear about the leaky bucket
how can i fetch water when it's frozen
how can i make coarse tea without water

help . . . ma, help
i've burned my socks
it's not my fault
i was just warming my feet at the wood fire!

neue donau [the new danube]

in the past you could have purified
yourself every ten miles down the road
whenever you tripped
you always managed to improvise a roll-over
baby titanoboas didn't need a passport
until they were seventy thousand years old

now you are a river for want of a bigger boat

if not for your bends, you would have been
the most celebrated night-crosser they'd ever known
the most august tale of rustic to rags
a fuller on a double-edged sword
a snail trail down a windowpane
a royal ballet soloist or forewoman in a paper mill
a twelve-hour shift en pointe
work calories for maintenance calories
just another pasture for leisured goats

they will probe your depths and shallows
they will slow your swifts
they will widen your defiles
don't flinch, you must remain in your quietude
they simply want to make you feel at home in their home
this, they insist, is for your own good

from your black forest source to your black sea mouth
they will want to know
how many iron gates you've lowered yourself through
how can you be so perfectly bruised
so imperfectly youthful

akdeniz [the white sea]

to a worm's eye
you are the wavy mountains of ararat
to a vulture in the sky
you are a camel carcass
drifting past the pillars of heracles

i get shell-shocked on your turquoise coasts
i get chest-trapped by your *hammam*
i get whip-creamed by your *nazar* socks
i get waylaid on your new vieux port

marcian had no regal pretense
he has been crowned by chance and chance alone
cleopatra at the temple of hathor
the wail of your children trapped in a catacomb
a wreath of olive leaves for a laurel forest
a piece of naïve art on latin skin
a stradivarius with spider-silk strings
she sings in the sunny key of palermo

your butchers licensed for the road
your physicians licensed for the press
your commanders licensed for the parliament
your belly-dance skirt gathers dust
your miniskirt gathers ghosts

your no sounds maybe
your maybe sounds yes
your yes sounds no
if there is no venom left
departure is your ultimate weapon

the fairy chimneys of anatolia
they no longer smoke

urban renewal

double or nothing, you and your hybridism
your face needs to be lifted, the sprawl beyond
your subconscious needs to be gentrified, the landfill
shall be renamed goldengarbageland, dig tunnels for
an extensive subway network for your pigeon
commuters, the public transport in your brain should
be integrated, a fence for hate padlocks right in front
of the white wedding chapel, graffiti shall be encouraged
on the inner walls of your empty chest, dog parks for dogs,
amusement parks for amusements, child-friendly facilities
for the parents of children who may never grow up,
bingo halls for all ages and sexual preferences, clear the
woods on the city's fringes for nine-hole golf courses,
logging shall be licensed to make way for streamlined
taxiways for international arrivals, plant garden plants
in every department store, to age is to get less serious
about life, to die is to be incinerated to be reincarnated,
a multi-purpose stadium for metal concerts and the
vipassana for the masses, two ivory chopsticks shall
be contracted to conduct the people's symphony orchestra,
a brand-new opera house to be modeled after a durian
shall be named after our own houseman, a nine-lane
boulevard of broken bones shall be the city's artery,
hotbeds will be moved to the outskirts, council houses
will be patched up with thatches, aquatic centers for those
who will learn to splash, splash and splash, waves of all sizes
shall be regenerated and recycled, the monument of doubt

in the plaza shall be torn down, in its place the leaning tower
of certainty will be erected, crocodiles shall be released in
the moat of the pentagonean presidential palace,
all administrative quarters of your soul shall be made
soundproof to prevent the intrusion of street noises
malling, walling, enthralling and everything else
that will make your cosmopolis
your über-capital

faddish sugar crystals

what about
the flip-flap of a lady's sarong
for alternative music
condensed f-words from a cup of tea
artificially-colored *pausis* replicated like reproduction art
art reproduced in formaldehyde
a roadside teashop, ants on jackboots
with our mouths agape, the longish
hand of a rickety old lady droops
as she bends over backward to
pick up a patinated shilling
the last remnant of the great war
the streetlamp limps in light rose red
the flap-flap of a hand fan
insects swarm in swarm behavior
a six-door black cadillac swooshes past
fumes shoot up and deflower the sky
fliers, handouts and fliers
fliers, fliers and more fliers

permanent installations

[untitled]

untattooed thighs
climb up the tower of babel
once a prince, now *pawrithada bilu,*
he threatens to devour his old servant *dathaka*
will he find his master a human victim
no redemption whatsoever
no moral there

[the butterfly effect]

the snake is starving
the snake attack frightens the frog
the frog croak causes the rain
the rainfall multiplies the sandflies
the sandflies drive the water buffalo to wallow
the wallowing buffalo scares the fish
the fish splash calls the paddy bird
the perching bird bends the butea tree
the perching bird bends the butea tree

[water color]

a water color
to save my labor in pure white

listen, another silent night
the saline flavor in the breeze
salting all the oysters of the seas
the eye of a vortex is her achilles' heel
the roars of the stars are deafening
waves, however wayward,
will wash up on the shore eventually

what of the hurricane lantern
the oil has run out
the wick has burned down
breathing a lungful of oxygen
the flame leaps up
to lick the luscious earth
for the very last time

[fox sighting]

a fox on a suburban path at midnight
her elegant furry tail trailing along like a comet
her pointed head hanging low
heading for earth like a comet
her cautious glance as captivating as a comet
there is more to both of us than meets the eye

[thorny devils]

lovers dovetailed
amoral amore stickier than banyan sap
after the disappearing act
enters a thief called grief

for having a light of her own
i have worshipped
an evanescent glowworm over the moon
don't consecrate my parched heart
you don't want to thrill
divine thorny devils
on that barren hill

coup d'état

attention!
salute!

blow the barrelled weapons
you are supposed to be on your knees
these greens are above politics
they have a plot, they have history

report to them your guest list
they will safeguard your wish list
with effect from today, all organs of states, divisions,
townships, wards and village-tracts are dissolved
they will whitewash dogfruit trees and stupas
they will eradicate opium and gambling
between should-be and is
they will lay a kissable road overnight
after breaking the dawn with dynamite
they will return to their barracks

comrades-in-arms are never at ease
they wish they didn't have to drill
left, right, left, right, left, right . . .
non-disintegration of the union
non-disintegration of national solidarity
perpetuation of national sovereignty
killer heels stomp off in army chic
left, right, left, right, left, right . . .

sad [seasonal affective disorder]

how may i help you, sir

may i remind you that the hand in glove that
knocked on your fitting room at closing time is
the hand of the cleaning agent that might help

nothing gift-wrapped for christmas
post-christmas is desirable

don't call me love
i won't buy it

would you consider this, sir

with every purchase
a 2-inch extension and 10 percent
increase in circumference for free

go away, will you

the futility of collecting things and
competition in compliment

lady's fingers

for those biochemical
flowers, her rhyme fingers
are to blame, in the swiftness
of arctic terns they swoop down
on their prey, her unmollifiable claws
take no prisoners   her senseless salmons
            never stray far from their death trap / their home
            brute phalanges always creep up to saliva nests
highly knuckled, lowly accentuated extremities
digits that can't be taught to count
those tentacles never prophesize
the tips of her left wing bloodied
by eight savage strings of life
big bolts in big aviaries
in search of big skies

how to roast an osturducken [and get away with it]

if you want to cook it, cook it
there's more to life than politics!
a monitor lizard is not a crocodile
a turkey is not an ostrich
turduckens for thanksgivings
osturduckens for bigger thanksgivings
no need to thank me
you need an ostrich, a turkey, a duck, a chicken and lots of guts for this dish
don't be so chicken-hearted
you don't blame shampoo for being anti-dandruff
you don't blame a buck's scrotum for flip-flopping
a clove or two, garlic always smells the same
there are those who kill three birds for one piglet
there are those who whale blue whales
and what of those who have poisoned mímir's well
you can do it
it doesn't take a chef's certificate from the department of vociferous *bain-marie*
defeather and debone birds
keep the feathers for your sofa
save the bones for soup
roast in time, toast in time
the jury will be out in front of the grandfather clock
my mouth will water with the combined appetite of
seventy-five thousand famished ghosts
just make sure
herbs, weeds, wine, bread and butter
all ingredients are local, organic and fresh
all ambrosial delights are free range and humanely executed

i swim

what an evolutionary impairment
to emerge is to submerge to submerge is to submerge
what an onus to resurface every now and then to take a deep breath
i know i swim well i know i swim with style
just one thing, i haven't yet learned to hide my dorsal fin
once i gave my kickboard to a little goby who'd forgotten her floats
i've once been netted, bycatch in a school of shrimps
i thought i'd kicked the ice bucket [now i shun nets, and schools of shrimps]
those who love me love me too much, those who hate me hate me just enough
there's nothing where the sky and sea met
i'm not a pentamerous starfish
a distressed dolphin
not a mucusy kokopu, spineless jellyfish
nor a stargazer from the seabed
i'm not an ayu to be salted and grilled
not a sting ray, nor a false moray
i don't know how to blow like a puffer
i don't come from endangered tuna
i don't associate with the wanton perch of warm currents
i can't be boxed like a molly
i won't bring luck like a feng shui carp
i don't mind being held up by rainbow reefs
i don't want to go extinct like a phantom shiner
i don't want to be pickled like a herring
i don't want to spawn like a clownfish
i don't want to go home like a salmon into the paws of a grizzly bear
i try to stay in my own lane
i won't piss in the puddle

fuck me untied

are you one of those who will import
our rice so you can bomb our village
you believe in the charity of your moneyed class
now that my body is stuck in your bottleneck, there is
no spillover effect, save for your sperm

i don't miss trains, they never come
i no longer trust the public ride
faced with the leviathan, i will be playing possum
lying low like a benthic fish, if not committing
another suicide

according to the buddha,
"hunger is a hot potato you always
want to throw at someone else,
you are the one who gets burned"

in your diplomatic dictum
there is no such thing as *mettā*, disinterested love
rain on a sunny day brings prowlers
you don't lecture on navigation to a crocodile king
you don't lead a monk in the way of scripture

your language suits you smart
your rhetoric shapes your mouth
your discourse waxes your moustache, your
sweet monologues mold your lips, mint your tongue

and cheapen your kisses into *bout de papier*
if, to you, "to untie" means "to fuck"
you don't have to untie me
just fuck me untied

after "the lie of art"

i hate walls that have eyes
i hate eyes that have walls
i hate seas without deep sea fish
i hate deep sea fish without seas
i hate free will without programming
i hate programming without free will
i hate siege mentality with historic predeterminism
i hate mental siege with prehistoric determinism
i hate inner path without intellect
i hate intellect without inner path
i hate life for reproduction's sake
i hate reproduction for life's sake
i hate industry for production's sake
i hate production for industry's sake
i hate charity for celebrity's sake
i hate celebrity for charity's sake
i hate art for people's sake and life-delimits-art
i hate people for art's sake and art-delimits-life
i hate mutual exclusivity
i hate exclusive mutuality
i hate the red-billed chough who only praises the crow
i hate the crow who only praises the red-billed chough
i hate language as a weapon of the powerless
i hate weapon as the language of the powerful
i hate translations from literals
i hate literals from translations
i hate hates that won't go away

i hate loves that stay
i hate to split pennies
i hate pennies that split
i hate eroticism without oral sex
i hate oral sex without eroticism
i hate pills before bedtime
i hate bedtime before pills
i hate clutter in the closet
i hate closets in the clutter
i hate yours truly
i hate truly yours

hallowe'en

you ooze with pus and buzz with flies
your aftershave smells like the autumn of death
you've sacrificed your legs for your land
you've travelled everywhere
you play sax in a supergroup
you play polo in sussex
you loop the loop better than the looper
you know how to hold your blood bottle
you chew with your mouth shut
you digest everything extremely well
you are faithful to your spouse
you like being with children
you know all the important phantasms
you are nice to your parents
you work out like an inbred lab mouse
you speak with the right accent
you work pro bono, you pay tax
you know how to press a dart
you even understand my language, *perkele!*
it's harrowing to see you, mr . . . ?
oh yes! your servant passed me your calling card
are you related to that war hero, *that* senior general?
of course, of course, your name does bring a well
to general clément von kafka-dome
good health, hardiness, and headlines
you've been such a warm corpse

your lips soft-spoken, your handshakes polished
your tipples plush, your manner gracious
now let me deseed you for your jade eyes
full of life, fleshy, human

blindfolded brahmins

a team of brahmins with impaired vision examines the royal white elephant . . .

[brahmin the biologist happens to feel the trunk and passes his judgment]

fuzzy-furred, red-eyed, wet-nosed, and tactile
it's not an ingrown toenail, it's not a french poodle, it's not a walrus
it has excellent olfactory perception
it has a pair of blowholes on its head

this serpent knows how to slither down a snake pit
how to pace up and down the eyebrows of society
how to steal up on an oiled bamboo pole, how to logroll, how to spell

i'm not talking about my eldest son
gentlemen, what we have here is a pachyderm
a very, very delicate animal

[brahmin the numerologist holds the tusks in his hands and delivers
his assessment]

these two enormous phalli are genuine godsends
they are as sharp as the number 8, as silky as 8
as generously proportioned as 8
as reassuring as the number 8 . . .

8 or killjoy
8 is the repository of sacred wisdom
8 is the lucky number for growth
8 is above karmic consequence
8 is for elected, eight is for re-elected
8 is blue cheese in the southern hemisphere
8 is fish paste in the northern hemisphere
8 is a big push, eight is perpetual peace
8 can protect you from four sorts of harm
8 can deliver you from five types of foes
8 can bring you all two thousand spices
8 will bless you with thirty-eight auspices
8 thousand dollars a month, fine by me

[brahmin the economist bumps into the elephant's tummy]

ceteris paribus, it may be a bull, it may be a bear
it may be a free rider in free trade for a free lunch
this means the mean reversion may or may not be inevitable

if corruption is her comparative advantage
we are a pack of complementary goods to this wholesome mammal
it's full of animal spirits and antitrusts, within the limits
of bounded rationality, it might or might not behave as i expected

shall we call it a colossal contagion, just like us,
this monster has stomached so many moral hazards
then again, in the long run we all are dead

[brahmin the commander sniffs around the elephant's hindquarters]

if it feels like a trojan horse, if it stinks like a trojan horse
if it quacks like a trojan horse, it is a trojan horse

— oppose those relying on external elements, acting as stooges, holding negative views
— oppose those trying to jeopardize the stability of the state and progress of the nation
— oppose foreign nations interfering in internal affairs of the state
— crush all internal and external destructive elements as the common enemy

deny, delay, deceive, disrupt, destroy
uphold the national cause, get ready for a total people's defence

[the brahmin who is never there]

thank you for your message, i am currently out of the office
i will get back to you as soon as possible

a walk with history

for maung tha noe

how do you write history
in a language that has no
past tense?

i don't ask for it
more than once
history stumbles over me

how is it that you are part of history
if you haven't fine-dined with her?

it was the railroad worm in adam's apple
it was the pine bark turned into rye bread
it was the rotten meat ration on the battleship potemkin
it was a hike in the price of oil
it was a viss of rice for a lot of vice
it was the iron chef in hell's kitchen at fuli restaurant

what's up in your hometown?

a turnpike,
a flyover is under construction
over the juncture of history

when did clio land?

this morning, about half past two

did she have anything to declare?

nothing
they strip-searched her anyway

what did they find on her?

a whistleblower, a conch-shell blower
a critically endangered cheroot industry
a pair of cheap putsches
the crowd psychologist dr. state with
his twin sons, racism and reverse racism
an albino cockroach, a fake hypocrite, and
an immigrant, whose name
you will never get

myanma: a collage

1.

the road to mandalay
is paved in good intentions
oh . . . no! not again!
they've come for us down from yunnan!

2.

we the *myanma*
we, the people of *mettā*,
do love our neighbors
if you want to grab my *inngyi*
you can have my *longyi*, too

3.

you, the hesperian,
yes, you, who is more papal than the pope,
uncork your burma campaign champagne
write up your visions, missions, and donation pleas
suit up and seal your accounting deals

come ye all, com' on,
let's save fish from drowning
let's feel the rhythm of burmese history
let's speak for *myanmapyi*
for the loveliest thing alive
for the festive jolly race
there's space for everybody

4.

the conflict is institutionalized and intractable
but it's not ideological
for it's been a sputter for survival
between the imagined community
the *tatmadaw* of the legitimacy hopeless and
the unimagined community
the diaspora of the integrity hopeless
hell is for the rest

5.

inside the country, everything is broken
everything is a catastrophe
no, no . . . probably not the thug force
and their self-serving cartography
no, certainly not the spirit of the lady
and not the chained gang
condemned to be free

6.

people's desire is their flight of fancy
if not their flight to safety
we wish to see *mizzima*
in *the new plight of myanmar*
the post-myanmar times in *the new era* and
the undamming of *the irrawaddy*

7.

repeat after me
"non-disintegration of the union,
non-disintegration of national solidarity
perpetuation of national sovereignty"
non-constitution, non-election, non-ceasefire
non-process, non-event, nonsense,
non grata, naypyidaw,
the most gilded kleptopolis in world history
....
one more non sequitur, no sweetener, please!

8.

don't you fret, you myanma,
don't you dawdle downing tea
democracy will come, don't you see
one day one fathom, bagan won't flee

cut

we owe them nothing
they didn't invent the alphabet
uphold the national objectives
wipe them out from the face of the planet, cleanse them
off all the known and unknown universes for good measure
here are the four cuts they must have

— cut their food
— cut their funds
— cut their recruit
— cut their intelligence

cut in the name of god
cut in the name of growth
cut in the name of a diamond jubilee
cut for the sake of love
cut, it doesn't cut it

come on, let's be honest
now that your misappropriation case seems to have tailed off
can you become more transparent than the malt whisky in your glass
look . . . there are fifty-five million poets earnestly
awaiting a payoff in your country
cut

they attempted to pickaxe her out of the cancer
they said it'd extend her life for one month

she only wanted an assisted suicide
by the time she left
there were two supernovas for her breasts
cut

cut because you are whatever you are
out of the earth you came as sharp as a bamboo shoot
as blunt as a mushroom, or twirled and twisted like a bean sprout
big-headed but just one among a million equally big heads
because you happen to be in season and you also happen to be
a snappy-springy asparagus

cut the crap
mango doesn't complement dal when you have diarrhea
i only let you hold my hand and you wanted to touch my lips
you can't leapfrog over a chasm
february brings on the sniffles, and june, light drizzles
castor-oil plant is always king in the jungle of weeds
cut the crack

i tell you what
if you finger a wet socket
you'll be electrocuted
if you divide 22 by 7
it will never end

my generation is best

childhood past life, polio sister, measly brother, river blindness,
tetanus twitch, bookworm, hookworm, head louse, earthworm,
over-baked marshmallow, sunburned matchstick, the posh leech who
loved to feast on ulcers, seven-year itch and whatnot warts, bliss it was
playing football in the downpour with those low-income diseases
isn't your generation best

in an expanding universe, we must be falling more and more apart
are you still a nightmare to your quarters, have you recovered from
your post-traumatic disorder, from being flogged, stripped naked and
tied up to the school flagpole for spoofing your national anthem,
from being jailed three years after being mistaken for a member of
the diamond marble syndicate for your unhealthy long hair, didn't you
also get eight months extra for being caught red-eared, listening to the
stones while stoned, you were a destructive element

there was no income inequality in your days, everyone was equally poor
no capital flight, there was no capital
no brain drainage in the decolonizing sewage system
the server was never down, there was no server
student radicals wore war-paint, not business suits
men didn't have to commit drunken suicide in *ressentiment*
they died young for a greater cause in the anti-imperialist struggle
women didn't have time to fight for their rights, they were
always kept busy breastfeeding babies in the kitchen
the government never needed to justify its policies through
pro-government policy think-tanks to appease the west

the state was madly prescient
when you were a lad, you said, poor prostitutes were routinely rounded up, rich ones were known as concubines or kept ladies, karaoke bars and korean soap-star lookalikes weren't rampant, race riots were routine, heroin addicts got harsh jail terms with hard labor, drug kingpins returning to the legal fold became philanthropists, the kgb antennae and the tendrils of local spies entangled, the cia weren't everywhere, brussels wasn't a bloc of eurocrats, washington wasn't a consensus

in those days, the air was still breathable, the jungles were
so thick they were untrekable, you could drink from any creek or river
mountains were still wholesome blocks of un-mined earth
if you didn't like your government party, you could always become a maoist rebel, or be labelled a pro-american felling axe, everything was black and white, your vision was never blurred, reality didn't have to be augmented

imagine, your composers, if their fingers weren't tuned in
diatonic harmonic hierarchy, would devastate a thousand john cages, your poets, if their conscience wasn't ideologically castrated, would chill a thousand allen ginsbergs to the bones, your painters, if their canvases weren't narrowly framed for the shortage of canvas and paint, would stir a thousand andy warhols to burn their life's work in frustration, your filmmakers, if their viewfinders weren't glued to moscow montage, would reduce a thousand woody allens into an insignificant heap of shame
. . . and you yourself, if and only if . . .

yes, yes . . . i dig you, stop weeping . . .
your generation is best

no football color

it's good
not to understand the circumstances
not being able to grasp the fourth-language commentaries
why they always throw pain across the pitch
right into your chest
or how they shin you even in injury time
what a turf specialist has to say about the carpet or
how humidity affects your footsie!
when men are numbered 0 to 10
man resorts to paraphilia
man turns into a character actor
salary commensurate with skill
a french knife can cut through swiss cheese no sweat
but isn't football, being football,
an extraordinarily roundish thing,
shouldn't the referee always trust her linesman?
you don't want to harp on about bach to a buffalo
you can't explain law 11 to an uninitiated
you can't unscore your own goal
i regret to inform you
you have everything but leg luck
the principle of short passes works
only when you are well-linked,
and wicked

timely applause and toothy smiles

now a carrot, now a cane
now you see it, now you don't
a well-hung knight in broad daylight
ranks, gambits, fool's mates, positional plays
upper house and lower house male bonding
ladies and gentlemen, distinguished white elephants
eminent hierophants and esteemed sycophants
a big hand to this succulent and jazzy watermelon
she has hurled stones at hot air balloons miles high
she has hauled cargo with the royal barge, she has
yachted around the world in her porcelain tub
for her peccadilloes, she'll be quartered
the central square is too crowded
too many monkeys, too many middlemen
the hostages are in, the queen is pinned
not all fruits sweeten as they ripen
i am a chilli, you are a lime
bitter gourds are other people
the empire is overstretched
the emperor is overdressed
denizens wear nothing but the loincloth
of law, it's no progression, a draw

corpse flower blooms in washington

what an ill omen!
what a good omen!

this voodoo lily blooms
when the bodhisattva is awakened!
when the end is nigh!
when the seed is sown!
when the coast is clear!

to sponge with it!
her stench takes you to fetid human flesh in syria
that will take you to summer roadkill in lapland
that will take you to putrefied fish pickle in the delta
that will take you to places between his toes

floriculturists call her deformed dick
she calls herself cassandra

the mandalay gazette 1885

women continue to gaze west and walk east
men, when soused, croon tom jones' *sex bomb* on karaoke,
when sober, tom waits' *better off without a wife*
scam and flimflam duel in a gory sword fight
tattooed members of the missing pinky gang haunt korean restaurants
privacy remains the biggest issue, even in the outhouse
as amateurish bigwigs go clownish willy-nilly
professional jesters get in-your-face-under-your-belly
more than ever, tv antennae cables are in demand for suicide by hanging
soft-voiced armenian cemetery makes tourists wish for death
fire escape ladders are lethal whenever they collapse
a mort floats in the palace moat, still smoking a havana
researchers identify three types of power-outage stress disorder
type-a complains all the time
type-b does nothing about the outage, and
type-c is above the outage
a gold medal in badminton and ping-pong
doesn't make you a tennis champion, claims a sport scientist
locals continue to fear the nearer sword
the poor eat dogs and the rich worship them
in business quarters, only unwrinkled yen are legal tender
foreign investment law asks investors to outjesus the jesus
thou shall not steal, thou shall not outburmese the burmese
true believers no longer know what comes first in their faith
the mad monk or the flighty boat
the porous border or the birth rate

the whoring media or the pimping state
buddha, dhamma or *sangha*
father, daughter or holy spirit
buy me, get my country free

pyongyang people's daily

as applications pile up for the prestigious
trophy tray bearer position for
the annual *kavya* academy gala
a horde of speech writers who thought
they were about to go ogle has been crushed to death
in a stampede for the best seat
"powered by the poor, we've now come
to a stage where progress is irreversible"
my feet can put up with forty-five brushes
by a tiger-tongue sandpaper but not once with that kind of lick by a lab
as someone who loves money as much as poetry
and who has neither
her motto has always been
"the *muu* may be just a rivulet but even the mighty nile fears her flash/floods"
since the state has appropriated her line into one of their economic objectives
she has taken up a new shibboleth
"what's important is important"
another potentially significant brawl
between two software engineering students
is about to take place in an insignificant internet café
"shed your secret skin!"
"leave your patriotic body!"
onlookers online who look forward to
onlooking a mass uprising are thoroughly disappointed
when a timely blackout shuts down the spit-spat
the crowd disperses as some of them go back to
gossiping about their neighbors or watching football

some of them leave the scene to serenade their lovers with
"apologies" by victory moon
the rest simply move on to watch the premiere,
"now your pretty hands, next your pretty cheeks"

child corpses

dead
children
are
easy
they aren't choleric
they don't leave wills
a child casket
is a light load
if a coffin is a fancy
infant death
agrees
with
a cardboard box or
a blanket
in
mass
graves
children
rest
more peaceable
than
parents
kids who were walked
into the gas chamber
thought
they were having
a meal

after a shower
untroubled
children
are
from six months on
most
babies
are capable of
sleeping
through
the
night

the 5000th

january
one
two
three
let's count
there were tanks
there were snipers
there were heads
there were bodies
forty-eight
forty-nine
fifty
and counting
there were commotions
there were other things to attend to
there were condemnations
there were concessions
there were other wars
there were other springs
where were we
ninety-eight
ninety-nine
one hundred
there were murderers
there were thugs
there were heads
there were bodies

there were potential peace laureates
there were martyrs
there were emergency closed-door meetings
there were rebel armies
there were public debates
there were policy deliberations
there were strategy statements
there were sanctions
august
they had reshuffled the cabinet at home
they had formed a parallel government in exile
there were more meetings
there were more campaigns
there were more concerns, more lobbies, more statements, more sympathies
nine-hundred and ninety-eight
nine-hundred and ninety-nine
one thousand
there was more news, more no-news, more news-news
there were raiders
there were rapists
there were trained assassins
there were butchers
there were prisoners of conscience
there were prisoners of sub-conscience
there were spies, there were stooges
there were negotiations
there were heads
there were bodies
there were heads of children on their mothers' bodies
there were voiceless protests by headless bodies

there were headless protests for voiceless bodies
december
four-thousand-nine-hundred and ninety-eight
four-thousand-nine-hundred and ninety-nine
five thousand
concerns get more profound
prayers get more desperate
there were more candles at candlelight vigils
their faces get more serious on tv
it's a crime against humanity
it's a crime against crime against humanity
it's a crime against crime against crime against humanity
by the way, where were we?
let's do it all over again
january
one
two
three

i told you there's a fire

what's the difference between a temporary
camp and an emergency camp, this is going
to be an in-depth interview, the lighting isn't
that good here, could you move a little over
there, the connection is bad, can you speak
louder please, hello, hello, hello, what a bummer,
this has to go online this evening, we've gotta
be ahead of them, how many children, how
many adults, how many women, how many
men, the death tally must be accurate, is this one in
any causal relation with past communal clashes, is there
any instigation, did you say you had to flee for your life
with all your ancestors and descendants on your shoulders,
members of police and armed forces, rescue and
rehabilitation committees, since the gentlemen in
sunglasses came by helicopters, that line sounds
good, don't miss it, in south african tradition, damn it,
this keyboard is stuck when i need it most, do you
really long for law and order of the past, can't they
do anything about rule of law, is that simply the
rage of the dispossessed, this time even the wildcat
fell victim to a forest fire, according to the report by
the investigation commission, you can't speak as a
mob, you can't speak as an individual, you can't speak
at all, lootings are common, someone must have thrown
things together, latrine problems, we've been squatting
here since the middle ages, just when my business was

taking off, this shall be our nation until the earth shatters
into bits, i've donated more than 40 lakh, no apartheid
at all in the distribution of rice, cooking oil, potato, salt
and fish paste, look . . . they are handing out food packets,
why don't you stay for lunch?

the rain maker

switch off the lights, turn the projector on
sit back and relax, let's enjoy the mirages
on *kayan* rice wine and cheese crackers

a few simple rules here
you may bite the hand that feeds you,
just don't feast on it
don't multitask if you don't know
how to run north for a southbound hare
don't kill two robins with one word
if you don't know how to lie to one of them
don't chew the shoes and the drapery
don't be a member of any poetic community

don't be a rose fancier
you don't want to be another down comforter
fine feathers are unfit for us humans
they make you too hot within
too cold without

look how the dormant underdog,
taken for granted rotten-dead,
has sprung back to life on *dukkha* media!

sickened with divided attention disorder
it jumps over the crown, chokes and
strangles the aristocratic order

the kingdom now needs a flea leap forward
the newly elected leader may be comely
just don't expect her to change the clime

isn't it fascinating?
how each and every cowry trapped in a hollowed-out bamboo
houses an entire symphony orchestra

anxiety attack

just like your father, grandfather,
great-grandfather, and great-great-grandfathers
with your whale skeleton
you will fill a museum
from your first baby cry to your last breath
every detail of you will be laid bare
dissection of your skin color, or your sex life
should give them a surprise or two
why you used this oar for that meander
who planted bad medicine in your path
how you might look without props or specs
your entire career has been dedicated to
nothing, but begonias, dahlias and petunias
future generations will be overwhelmed
they will probably appreciate different messages
inherent in the different patterns of different
longyis you wore to different functions—a new
longyi, or two, each day with a perfume to match
how your not-so-sweet-not-so-sour smiles
lifted one land and lanced another
researchers will no doubt nose into your diaries
your pots and pants will reveal how you have been
a product of contingencies, exigencies, context or karma
that's why, they will explain, like your ancestors,
you were entitled to particular upcountry fragrant rice
steamed in a particular manner in a particular bowl
kept warm with top and bottom charcoal fire

not to mention
your penchant for postmodern platform flip-flops!
from different premises
people, long after your departure, will die arguing
how your life has been
history's greatest success, or
its most dismal failure

faith supper

claptrap/cream pie
sweetmeat/moonshine
landscape/portrait
bottom-up/top-down
home-grown/half-done
board game/cheetah
pomegranate/fruit cake
bipolar/disorder
guest list/gatecrasher
fuzzy logic/set theory
woe gone/animal party
vain vanity/big burp
dress code/putrid parody
for/get every thing
just bring your own scenery

the burden of being *bama*

it's living on
sawdust and shrimp paste
to save for diamonds

it's being a lustrous luna
in a bamboo tube
thinking "how dainty i am!"

it's being a haystack fire
flaring suddenly
fading out swiftly

it's aching for the aunt
from the embrace of the mother

what's your key
majority in minor-c or minority in major-d
ceasefire in flat-b or cease-identity in sharp-g
give me a falsetto
let's improvise
no need for harmony

what would you choose
want, rage or ignorance
defeatism or maldevelopment
an increase in viral load or a decrease in internet speed
sexual preoccupation or self-denial

power cuts or power crazes
a bag of rice or an ounce of democracy
myopic blitheness, escapist wizardry and alchemy
syncretization of incompatibilities
internalization of irreconcilabilities
the four noble truths
the four oaths.........
....
....
the menu is endless
the die's been cast

your karma is you
life short
suffering tall
plenty of water
no fish, no fish at all

no romance love

this is for you, yes, you
the bozogoon in rangoon yangon!
there's no romance love on the bus-car line-car
if you can't afford a steering-wheeled jalopy
don't bother with a three-wheeled sidecar
in your street corner falafel-seller's rag
don't ya come to windermere
you look like a spare's spare
a flip-flop thief in the dock
a platform hawker on the run
bride price is bloody high in my quarters
phayphay daddy says i mustn't marry down
maymay mommy says i can choose who i wish
but you, why you, and your caste,
phayphay maymay suggest,
i might as well consider a tailless terrier
a preschool baby costs cash money, 1,300 usd a month
with your invirile inkhorn income
you won't even get me to *thakayta*
look, i haven't seen my menses in six weeks
i don't really want a baby daughter
we need an air-conditioned nest
overriding concern is temperature

the day he regretted swimming butterfly [across the baltic with a beer can in his hand]

are you our member
would you like chips with your fish burger
why am i at one of those pearly gates restaurants
how pesky are afterlife insurance salespeople

what about a pair of goggles for your swimming trunks
for every off-center lid, there is an off-center pot
a toddy palm leaf, a perfect complement for a lightning rod
get a goat hide free with every purchase of a pet elephant
a ferry ticket for every hundred sin dollars spent
a safety net for vultures that tend to fall off bunk beds

happiness is best served at room temperature
[my room temperature, not yours]
it goes down really well with *dukkha*
[your *dukkha*, not mine]

muscle cramps drown even seals
always wear a life jacket
it's absolutely necessary

strawman story

i am going to rest
just a straw mat for my back
like a drowning man grasping a straw
socrates sips his poison through a straw
life is a squiggle drawn in the water with a straw
emptiness in form, form in emptiness in a straw
can anyone share with me her last straw
straw for the right, grass for the left
the winner is the loser in drawing straws
like a rabbit burrowing into a straw hat
i am going to nest
you can ring my bell anytime with a straw
in a strawy strawy night
in a world built with mud bricks without straw
i am a strawy-eyed owl
i suck up my strawberry brew with my built-in straw
not all the straws are straight
my veins are straws of blood
i was born in a barn of straws

strawman [in re-verse]

i was born in a barn of straws
my veins are straws of blood
not all the straws are straight
i suck up my strawberry brew with my built-in straw
i am a strawy-eyed owl
in a world built with mud bricks without straw
in a strawy strawy night
you can ring my bell anytime with a straw
i am going to nest
like a rabbit burrowing into a straw hat
the winner is the loser in drawing straws
straw for the left, grass for the right
can anyone share with me her last straw
emptiness in form, form in emptiness in a straw
life is a squiggle drawn in the water with a straw
socrates sips his poison through a straw
like a drowning man grasping a straw
just a straw mat for my back
i am going to rest

i've seen death

[april 2010]

my doctor said, "i don't know how long you will live . . ."
i didn't bother with the rest . . .
i've seen more death than money in life
be my guest if you've seen more cash than death

"death ain't matter, life ain't matter" to ma ei
zeyar lynn has been exiled from death
"death is just another room" blake said
orwell who had shunned a slow death died a slow death
sargon boulus has seen death "doing its ablutions in the public fountain"
i've seen death

[may 1974]

when i was a butterball with a big head
i came down with an infant sickness
my parents fenced me in from death
i bounced back from the shaman's lap
he pocketed his fee as he professed,
"the boy will live 120 years"

[march 1986]

i skipped school for a swim
in the tint of ocean blue
death came a knocking in the form of a dryad
in the violent creek
my limbs went vapid
my lungs breathed white waters like a glass sponge
whoever saved me
you owe me a death

[december 1996]

on a street to shwedagon in yangon
i faced off with death
death was a merciful baton
a bayonet would have been a better match
the sophistication of their repression granted me
just a glimpse of death

[october 2006]

this time
poteen and pearl flakes interlaced
i rubbed shoulders with death

death shit in my bed
death puked in my face

death left me utterly disgusted
death compromised was worse than death

[a while ago]

i chanced upon death in the whites of her orgasmic eyes
in her mortal embrace
death is love   death is hate
death is smart   death is disdain
death is daft   death is sense
death is senseless   death is essence
death is existence   death is alive
death is dead

water elephant

water elephants exist
or do they?
to every *mahout*
water elephants are real, and ethereal
in water, with fisheyes, they move like fish
on land they can survive for hours
they breathe through trunks
they are short, and plump,
with two pairs of legs,
each with four to five claws,
also known as minor tongues
when fully grown
miniature mammoths are about 0.25 mm
(0.009 in.) long and 0.2 mm (0.007 in.) high
they feed on water corn
they love water spinach
they wander underwater all day
they furrow your brow at night
elephas minimus are semi-nocturnal
they are particularly fond of translucent waters
of pikes, perches and pebbles
elephants, real or ethereal,
are never seen in water elephant habitat
instinct tells them—
water elephant bites fatal

monosodium glutamate

for zeyar lynn

it isn't sweet or salty
it isn't sour or bitter
it's somewhere in between
somewhere from above

it's umami
the savory delight of monosodium glutamate
the buddha's poop that has colonized our cuisines since 1908
the inducer of droll and drivel, that sensation of furriness on the tongue
the teaser to the throat, the softener to the hard palate
the loveless lover to the lingual tonsil
the made-in-japan-chinese-restaurant syndrome
the diamond powder, the tortoise hair, the hare horn
recognized safe for the general population
no serious adverse reactions
no long-lasting effects

only an imperishable aftertaste
from *myeik mohinga* to houston beef jerky
from *kaesŏng* instant noodle to lima *pachamanca*
from the shrimp cocktail of nasa astronauts in space to
the food-aid package in east africa
even the inuit imbue their whales, walruses and seals with an essence of taste
the seasoning for all seasons
the most addictive of additives

the non-essential you can't live without
the acid you yearn to lick every second
the undecided neurotransmitter
the enhancer of life's flavors
the condiment to contemporary conditions

no wonder then
99 percent of humanity is over-ajinomotoed
the rest is under-ajinomotoed
if you are a 1-kilogram rat
15 grams of the sweet dust is your lethal oral dose
it works 50 percent of the time

monsoon

mango cooler in the pantonal pipe
a latin lover for a moscow mule
chi chi attempts a crocodile bite
mary mudslides a planter's mash

skies redden and thicken—
el diablo imminent

seagrasses surge and swell
just one shell for two hermit crabs
sea urchin lights her aristotle's lantern
sand dollars turn sand castles into a sandstorm
joey disappears into his mother's chest

coconuts in the canopy kiss
get wet and freefall into the jungle
let's drift together, let's not drift apart
don't you whinge like a locked-out shepherd
haven't you seen a tidal resonance

encomium for mr. yew

mr. yew
i am in love with you
you are not common yew
you are not pacific yew
you are not mexican yew
you are not japanese yew
you are not canadian yew
you are not sumatran yew
you are not himalayan yew
you are mr. yew
you are above any poisonous yew that guards a church graveyard from cows
there has never been the like of yew
there never will be the like of yew
you are a perfect syncretism of heart and brain
yew heart in your brain
yew brain in your heart
yew is the peerless symbiosis of art and science
yew is the artful science
yew is the scientific art
yew has always been right
yew has always been left
yew has always been the middle
only yew knows where else
yew is supreme
yew is almighty
yew is omniscient
yew is omnipotent

your lordship won't dance your balls bounce for an ounce of yewlogy,
but nonetheless, your goodness,
let me rename your island of reclaimed land that is now inundating the mighty ocean the *yewland*
bless me with the honor of a pyramid for yewer grace
could i embalm yewer heavenly spirit's wholesome body
please allow me to encase yewer majesty's brainy heart
kindly let me enshrine yewer worship's hearty brain
bestow upon me a pickle of yewer divine entrails
could i forever venerate, praise and kowtow yewer holiness
my great guardian, my good shepherd
my jade-footed-sun-faced monarch of the universe
the owner of eighteen thousand gold umbrellas
and ninety-nine thousand white elephants
my king of kings, my most masterly master
the post-mortal and immortal you
mr. yew

cuban fish-head soup

never say no to her propositions
you wouldn't even know what hit you
she has the right to self-defense
the right to bare arms, legs without fishnet stockings
in the generosity of local fishermen
if she doesn't recall the name of your king
let her call him george the president
if she doesn't recall the name of your city
let her call it *varanasi*
if you don't want "apple tragedy"
don't menace her with your apple gun
something isn't better than nothing
lesser law isn't better than lawlessness
fifty isn't half as good as a hundred
if she spills words in your wonder alley
she'll lick them off with ei, ie or ai
her mother tongue is monosyllabic
her oral tradition is polytonal
if she ever gets to see tosca at the state opera
she will go home after the second act
she calls it justice done
she calls it the bloody end

Notes

to the navel of the earth

samsara [သံသရာ]: “continuous flow”, is the endless cycle of birth, life, death, rebirth and reincarnation in Buddhism and other Indian religions.

“right view, right intention, right speech, right action, right livelihood, right effort, right mindfulness, right concentration” are the noble eightfold path in Buddhism; only by following the noble eightfold path can one arrive at nirvana.

avīci well [အဝီစိတွင်း]: a drilled well, as opposed to a dug well; avīci wells are usually powered by jet pumps; from Sanskrit and Pali, “without waves”, it is also the lowest and most damning “non-returning” layer of Buddhist hell.

buddha, dhamma, sangha: the Buddha, his teaching and the Buddhist order of monks (and nuns)—the trinity of Buddhism.

panning for alluvial gold [at the confluence of her dreams]

The six glories of the Buddha are lordship (*issariya*), doctrine (*dhamma*), fame (*yasa*), eminence (*siri*), wish (*kama*) and endeavor (*payatta*).

padauk [ပိတောက်]: Also known as *amboyna*, is the flower associated with the Burmese new year. Padauk wood is valued for its durability.

thagyan [သင်္ကြန်]: *Thingyan*, the Burmese new year water festival that usually falls in April (from Sanskrit, meaning passage or transit of the old to the new).

yane [ယိမ်း]: a group dance usually performed by young women during celebrations such as the Burmese new year.

chaos clock

art: antiretroviral drugs

"Practice safe sex, prostitution is illegal in Myanmar" is an official piece of advice to tourists from the Myanmar Ministry of Hotels and Tourism, found in the pamphlet *Do's and Don'ts for Tourists: How Can You Visit Myanmar Responsibly* (2012).

ajinomoto: a Japanese food corporation that produces seasonings, cooking oil and other food products.

end of strife [ရန်ကုန်]: an English rendering of Yangon/Rangoon.

power light: the name of an upmarket Rangoon restaurant on the banks of Kandawgyi [The Royal Lake].

welcome to the fort town of ba htoo

tatmadaw [တပ်မတော်]: literally The Royal Armed Forces, the official title of the Myanmar Armed Forces.

tamain [ထမိန်]: a type of sarong worn by Burmese women.

dukkha [ဒုက္ခ]: a Buddhist concept that encompasses suffering, angst, anguish, frustration, pain, discontent, affliction, anxiety, sorrow, discomfort, stress, misery—the general burdens of life.

lawksawk

saopha [စော်ဘွား]: a royal title used by the hereditary rulers of the Shan State of Burma.

taung gyi (Taung Gyi): capital of the Shan state.

mawlamine (Mawlamine/Mawlamyaing): capital of the Mon state.

Willys: manufactured from 1941 to 1945, the Allied Forces introduced these military jeeps to Burma in World War II. Hundreds of decommissioned Willys ended up serving the Burmese armed forces after the War. Some of them are still running today.

phayagyi [ဘုရားကြီး]: the grand stupa; the oldest stupa in a town is generally referred to as the phayagyi.

tabota: a company that produces generators.

neue donau [the new danube]

Neue Donau: a site in Vienna.

akdeniz [the white sea]

akdeniz: (Turkish) The White Sea, also a common Turkish family name.

nazar socks: (Turkish) nazars are eye-shaped, blue handmade glass amulets believed to deflect the evil eye; children's socks printed with nazar eyes are common.

Marcian (392–457) was Byzantine Emperor from 450 to 457.

urban renewal

vipassana [ဝိပဿနာ]: contemplative or "analytical meditation" in Theravada Buddhism.

faddish sugar crystals

Taken from *The Funeral of the Rugged Gold (November 1996)*, a campus chapbook at the Yangon Institute of Technology. Translated and adapted from the Burmese by the author.

pausi [ပေါက်စီ]: *baozi* in Chinese, a common Chinese delicacy, steamed white bread dumplings filled with meat, vegetable or bean paste.

permanent installations

untattooed thighs [ပေါင်ဖြူ]: In pre-colonial Burma, it was customary for young men to have their thighs covered in tattoos. Just like entering monkhood, but no less significant, tattooing one's thighs marked coming of age. Highly stylized and sanctified thigh-tattoo figures vary from demons and wild animals to the Burmese alphabet framed in fist-sized oval traceries.

In Buddhist lore, King Pawrithada of the Kingdom of Varanasi got hooked on human meat after trying a dish prepared by his chef, Dathaka. The meat came from the body of a freshly executed criminal. Soon Dathaka found himself cooking the king's favorite human dish, using the flesh of condemned criminals, as the King did not like the more readily available flesh from those who had died of natural causes. When there were no criminals on the death roll, Dathaka resorted to killing innocent citizens to appease his master. More and more innocent citizens went missing. An emergency investigative committee discovered that the king had turned into a *bilu*, a cannibalistic ogre. Both King Pawrithada and his loyal chef were exiled. Once out of the kingdom, the king told Dathaka he would eat his own servant if he were to be deprived of human meat.

how to roast an osterducken [and get away with it]

mímir's well: Mímir or Mim, renowned for his knowledge and wisdom, is a figure from Norse mythology. Mímir attained great knowledge by drinking from his namesake well.

fuck me untied

mettā [မေတ္တာ]: a Buddhist notion, usually translated as loving-kindness, compassion or disinterested love.

after "the lie of art"

"The Lie of Art" is a poem by Charles Bernstein.

hallowe'en

perkele: also known as Ukko, is the chief god of the Finnish pagan pantheon. "Perkele!", when pronounced with an elegant rolling r, is an interjection akin to "Devil!" in meaning and "Fuck" in intensity.

a walk with history

fuli restaurant: a Chinese-Burmese restaurant on Insein Road, Yangon.

myanma: a collage

1\.

On the Road to Mandalay is the title of a popular song adapted from Rudyard Kipling's 1890 poem "Mandalay". The road to Mandalay in the poem refers to the famous waterway, the Irrawaddy, without which it would have been much more difficult for the British to occupy Burma in three phases from 1823 to 1886.

2\.

myanma here refers both to Burma and to an individual from Burma.

inngyi [အင်္ကျီ]: tunic, top or shirt.

longyi [လုံချည်]: Burmese sarong.

3\.

In *Saving Fish from Drowning* by Amy Tan, "a pious person said that he attempted to rescue fish from drowning by taking them out from the sea. When the fish expired, he was wise enough to sell them to make money for himself. Each time he repeated this activity, he claimed that he was saving fish from drowning."

Burma historian Michael Charney points out that continuity has characterized Burma throughout its history. Structurally, Burma has remained unchanged, despite vast experiences with colonization, decolonization and dictatorial rule since the late nineteenth century. In his own words: "The Burmese today are just as unhappy with their government as earlier generations; economic poverty continues to figure as prominently among Burmese concerns as it has any time in the past. Basic civil liberties are denied today as they were almost a half-century ago."

myanmapyi [မြန်မာပြည်]: The Union of Burma/Myanmar.

"the loveliest thing alive" is a line from George Orwell's "Ironic Poem About Prostitution" (ca. 1923).

4.

"imagined community" comes from the work of Benedict Anderson.

5.

"Everything Is Broken" is a song by Bob Dylan, and also the title of Emma Larkin's 2010 book: *Everything Is Broken: A Tale of Catastrophe in Burma.*

"The Lady" in the Burmese context usually refers to Daw Aung San Suu Kyi.

"Man is condemned to be free" is one of Jean-Paul Sartre's best-known aphorisms.

6.

Propaganda billboards advertising the "People's Desire" were a common sight in Burma from the 1990s to the early 2010s.

The New Light of Myanmar is the Burmese regime's daily paper.

Myanmar Times, the *New Era* and *The Irrawaddy* are the names of Burmese news journals operating within and outside of Burma.

7.

People's Desire [According to the State Peace and Development Council of Myanmar], the people of Myanmar should:

–Oppose those relying on external elements, acting as stooges, holding negative views;
–Oppose those trying to jeopardize the stability of the State and progress of the nation;
–Oppose foreign nations interfering in internal affairs of the State;
–Crush all internal and external destructive elements as the common enemy;
–Along with the "People's Desire", the "Three Main National Causes" are as follows:

–Non-disintegration of the union
–Non-disintegration of national solidarity
–Perpetuation of national sovereignty

The People's Desire and National Causes form the backbone of the Burmese regime's worldview and have been required printing on the opening page of every book, magazine and paper published in the country from the early 1990s to the early 2010s. They are also deeply embedded in the 2008 constitution of Myanmar.

cut

dal: a thick stew usually prepared from split pigeon peas or lentils, known as *pehin* [ပဲဟင်း]. In Burma, *pehin* is an important part of Burmese-Indian cuisine, and a staple for both the Burmese armed forces and prisoners.

pyongyang people's daily

kavya [ကဗျာ]: poem or poetry, the term originally referred to the Sanskrit literary style used by Indian court poets.

the rain maker

kayan: the Kayan are a subgroup of the Kayah/Karenni people.

the burden of being *bama*

Bama/Myanma is the majority ethnic group in Burma/Myanmar.

Maldevelopment: violation of the integrity of organic, interconnected and interdependent systems, which sets in motion a process of exploitation, inequality and injustice; the concept was introduced by Vandana Shiva in *Staying Alive: Women, Ecology and Survival in India* (1988).

The four oaths drilled into the conscious and subconscious of members of the Myanmar Armed Forces are as follows:

–We shall be loyal to the state and citizens;

–We shall be loyal to fallen *tatmadaw* members;
–We shall carry out the order and duty assigned from above;
–We pledge ourselves to sacrifice our life for our state, citizens and the *tatmadaw*.

no romance love

bus-car line-car: public transportation in Yangon/Rangoon.

sidecar: Burmese for trishaw.

Windermere: a gated community in Rangoon also kn own as Thanlwin Road.

Thakayta: Rangoon suburb.

water elephant

mahout: an elephant driver.

cuban fish-head soup

"Apple Tragedy" is a poem by Ted Hughes.

Afterword

ko ko thett is a poet by choice and a Burmese by chance. The poems in this collection, many of which have appeared in English-language literary magazines worldwide, range from "faddish sugar crystals," written in Burmese for his 1996 illegal campus chapbook at the Yangon Institute of Technology, to his autumn 2014 "anxiety attack" at the University of Leuven. Apart from his own work as a writer and translator, he is the co-editor and translator of the seminal volume *Bones Will Crow: 15 Contemporary Burmese Poets*, (ARC, 2012; Northern Illinois University Press 2013).

ko ko thett's poetry explores the possibility of the translatability of lived experience between the personal and the political, and the possibility of the mutual transferabilities between languages as disparate as Burmese, English and Finnish—as in "you even understand my language, *perkele*." The burden of being burmese is not just his. It is also yours.